What do you get when you cross an apple with a **Christmas tree**? And where do **snowmen** keep their money?

This tiny little book is PACKED FULL of cheesy **Christmas** jokes and gags – guaranteed to make you groan.

More bad jokes than a sledgeful of Christmas crackers!

PUFFIN BOOKS
Published by the Penguin Group: London, New York, Australia,
Canada, India, Ireland, New Zealand and South Africa
Penguin Books Ltd, Registered Offices: 80 Strand,
London WC2R 0RL, England

puffinbooks.com

First published by Puffin Books 1994
This edition published 2014
004

Made and printed in Italy by L.E.G.O. S.p.A

British Library Cataloguing in Publication Data
A CIP catalogue record for this book is available from the British Library

ISBN: 978–0–723–29671–3

RAYMOND BRIGGS

Father Christmas

CONTENTS

It's Christmas.

The busiest time of the year for me. It's work, work, work from the beginning of November right up to blooming Christmas Day. It's blooming miserable, I can tell you. So what I do to cheer myself up is tell myself jokes. Then I thought, there're a lot of people who need cheering up, too so why not share my favourite jokes with them?

Happy blooming reading!

CHRISTMAS CRACKERS

Where do ghosts go at
Christmas?

To a
phantomime

What do monkeys sing at
Christmas?

'Jungle bells,
jungle bells'

Knock, knock!

Who's there?

Mary!

Mary who?

Mary Christmas!

What's
Christmas
called in
England?

YULE
BRITANNIA

What do you get when you cross
an apple with a Christmas tree?

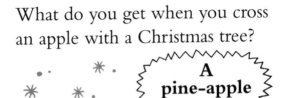

**A
pine-apple**

Which burns longer, a white
candle or a red candle?

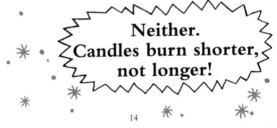

**Neither.
Candles burn shorter,
not longer!**

How can you tell
time with a candle?

Listen to the
candles-tick

What did the big
candle say to the
little candle?

I'm going
out tonight!

15

What did you
give your little brother
for Christmas?

MEASLES!

As shepherds washed
their socks by night,
All seated round the tub,
A great big bar of
soap came down
And they began to scrub.

What do you give
a train driver for
Christmas?

PLATFORM
SHOES

What did one Christmas cracker say to another?

A woman went to the pet shop to buy a parrot for her little girl for Christmas.

'I want a parrot for my little girl,' she told the man.

'Sorry,' said the man. **'We don't do swaps.'**

Why did Jimmy's aunt
knit him three socks
for Christmas?

**Because his mother
wrote and told her
he had grown
another foot.**

What happens if you eat
Christmas decorations?

**You get
tinselitis**

How do you feel
at Christmas?

Yule be happy

After eating a big Christmas dinner Peter went straight out to play. Half an hour later he came in, groaning and holding his tummy.

'**What's the matter?**' asked his mother. '**Are you in pain?**'

'**No,**' said Peter. '**The pain's in me.**'

Why are Christmas
trees like bad knitters?

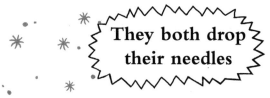

**They both drop
their needles**

What do sheep
sing at Christmas?

**Ewele-tide
carols!**

Do you like the dictionary
I bought you for Christmas?

**Yes, I do! I just can't
find the words to
thank you enough.**

What is the best Christmas
present in the world?

**A broken drum.
You just can't beat it!**

Who hides in the bakery
at Christmas?

A mince spy!

What do you call a
cat in the desert?

Sandy Claws!

What carol can you
sing in the desert?

**'O camel ye
faithful'!**

What do you get if you cross a bell with a skunk?

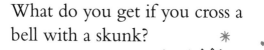

Jingle smells!

How many letters are there in the Christmas alphabet?

Twenty-five. There's no 'L'

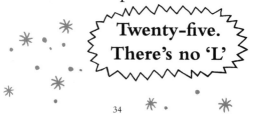

As shepherds watched
their flocks by night,
All tuned to BBC,
The angel of the Lord
came down,
And switched to ITV.

Books for Christmas:

Unusual Pets
by Terry Dactyl

Do It Yourself
by Andy Gadgett

Rice Growing
by Paddy Field

Keep Fit for All
by Horace Zontalbars

Swimming the Channel
by Francis Near

Simple Mathematics
by Algy Brar

Home Heating
by Arthur Mometer

Springtime
by Teresa Greene

Hark to the Singing!
by Harold Angels

The First Noel
by Carol Singer

DEER, DEER!

Why do reindeer wear fur coats?

Because they'd look silly in plastic macs

How long should a reindeer's legs be?

Long enough to reach the ground

What do reindeer hang on their Christmas trees?

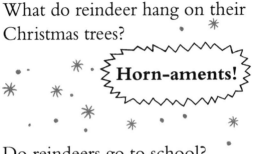

Horn-aments!

Do reindeers go to school?

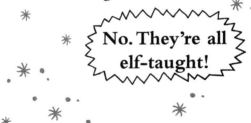

No. They're all elf-taught!

Why did the reindeer
wear black boots?

**His brown
ones were at
the menders.**

Where do you find reindeer?

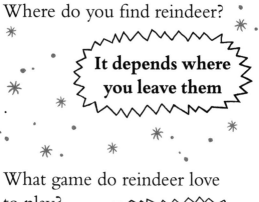

It depends where
you leave them

What game do reindeer love
to play?

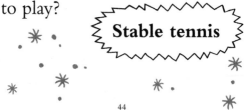

Stable tennis

Why did no one bid for Donner
and Blitzen at the auction?

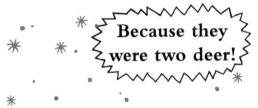

**Because they
were two deer!**

How do you make a slow
reindeer fast?

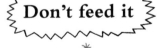

Don't feed it

Do you know
the story of
the three deer?

Dear,

dear,

dear.

There was a young
reindeer from Surrey,
Who cooked up a large
pot of curry.
He ate the whole lot,
Straight from the pot,
And ran to the tap
in a hurry.

What do you call a one-eyed
deer who lends a helping hand?

Good idea

What do you call a deer with
no eyes?

No idea

What do you call a deer with
no eyes, nose, ears or legs?

What is the
wettest animal?

**A
reindeer.**

What did Father Christmas do when the reindeer chewed his favourite book?

Took the words right out of his mouth

Why don't reindeer like penguins?

They can't get the wrappers off

Bet I can lift a reindeer
with one hand.

Bet you can't!

You're on. Show me a
reindeer with one hand
and I'll lift it for you!

How does a
reindeer get
down a tree?

**He sits on a
leaf and waits
for autumn.**

What do you do
with a blue reindeer?

**Try to
cheer
it up**

What do you do with a green
reindeer?

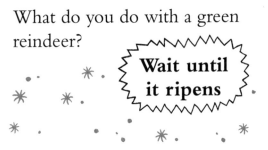

**Wait until
it ripens**

What do you get if you cross
a reindeer with a worm?

**Big holes in
the garden**

How many
legs does a
reindeer have?

Six:
fore-legs in front
and
two at the back.

What kind of
umbrellas do
reindeer use
in heavy rain?

Wet ones.

Why did the reindeer take a
ruler to bed with him?

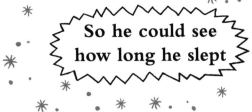

**So he could see
how long he slept**

How do you make a reindeer
fly?

**Buy it an
airline ticket**

What happened to the reindeer
who swallowed an Oxo cube?

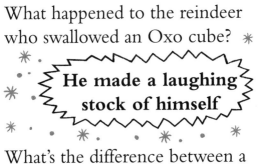

**He made a laughing
stock of himself**

What's the difference between a
biscuit and a reindeer?

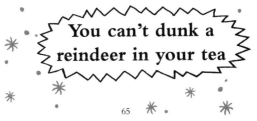

**You can't dunk a
reindeer in your tea**

Why did the
reindeer wear
sunglasses on
the beach?

**He didn't
want to be
recognized.**

IT'S SNOW JOKE!

How do you
know there's a
snowman in
your bed?

You wake up wet.

Which two letters of the alphabet do snowmen prefer?

I. C.

Where do snowmen keep their money?

In a snowbank

What athlete is warmest in winter?

A long jumper!

Why did the snow-drop?

Because it heard the cro-cus

What's it called
when two
snowmen fight?

An icebox.

76

Where does your mum come from?

Alaska.

Don't bother, I'll ask her myself.

What's a snowman's
favourite song?

**'There's no
business like
snow business'**

How did the snowman make anti-freeze?

He put ice-cubes in her bed

How did the eskimo find a way to keep the roof on his house?

Iglood it

What's ice?

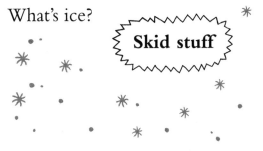

Skid stuff

How did the snowman keep himself cool at the football match?

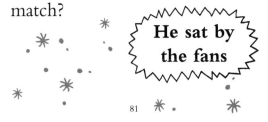

He sat by the fans

What did the
snowman order
at the café?

**Icebergers with
chilli sauce.**

How do polar bears see each other in all that snow?

They have very good ice sight

Do you think it's going to snow today?

It depends on the weather

What do you
call a penguin
in the
Sahara Desert?

Lost.

What's an ig?

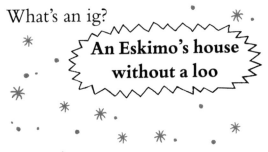

**An Eskimo's house
without a loo**

What do snowmen eat
for lunch?

Iceburgers

Where do snowmen go
to dance?

To snowballs

How does a snowman
travel around?

By icicle.

What sort of ball doesn't bounce?

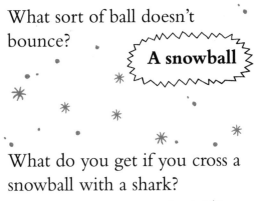

A snowball

What do you get if you cross a snowball with a shark?

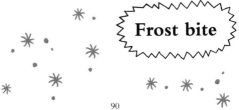

Frost bite

What do you call an Eskimo's cow?

An Eskimoo

What's the difference between an iceberg and a clothes brush?

One crushes boats and the other brushes coats

What stays
hot even at
the North Pole?

Mustard.

There was a young
fellow called Fisher,
who was fishing for
fish in a fissure,
when a seal, with a grin,
pulled the fisherman in;
now they're fishing the
fissure for Fisher.

What's white and goes up?

A silly snowflake

What fish do you need if you're on the ice?

Skate

What ship would you take to
a party?

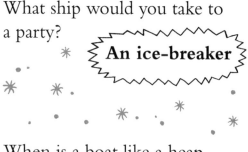

An ice-breaker

When is a boat like a heap
of snow?

**When it
comes a-drift**

FATHER CHRISTMAS

What do you call a man who claps at Christmas?

Santapplause

What do the reindeer sing to Father Christmas on his birthday?

Freeze a jolly good fellow

Why don't you ever see Father
Christmas in hospital?

**Because he has
private elf-care!**

Who is Father Christmas's
favourite singer?

Elf-is Presley!

What do you get if you cross Father Christmas with a detective?

Santa Clues.

Who says Oh, Oh, Oh?

Father Christmas walking backwards

What do you get if you cross Father Christmas with a duck?

A Christmas Quacker!

Twinkle, twinkle, chocolate bar,
Santa drives a rusty car,
Press the starter,
Press the choke,
Off he goes in a
cloud of smoke.

Why is a banana
skin like a jumper?

**Because
it's easy to
slip on.**

Why does Father Christmas
like to work in the garden?

**Because he likes to
hoe, hoe, hoe**

Who delivers presents to baby
sharks at Christmas?

Santa Jaws

What did Father Christmas say
when he won a saucepan in
a raffle.

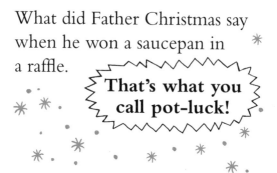

**That's what you
call pot-luck!**

Why did Father Christmas go
to the doctor's?

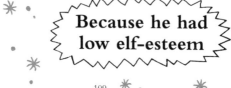

**Because he had
low elf-esteem**

Why do French
people eat snails?

**They don't like
fast food.**

What does Father Christmas
call his money?

Iced lolly

What is it called when Father
Christmas stops for a rest?

Santa Pause

What happens when Father
Christmas gets stuck in a
chimney?

He gets
Santa-Claus-trophobia!

Does Father Christmas enjoy
his work?

It has its ups
and downs

What's the best
thing to put into
a mince pie?

Your teeth.

What do you get if Father Christmas goes down the chimney while the fire is lit?

Krisp Kringle!

What goes red, white, red, white, red, white?

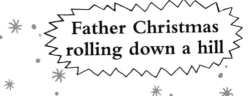

Father Christmas rolling down a hill

What's Father Christmas's
favourite pizza?

**One that's deep pan,
crisp and even**

What nationality is Father
Christmas?

North Polish

What's mad and
goes to the moon?

**A loony
module.**

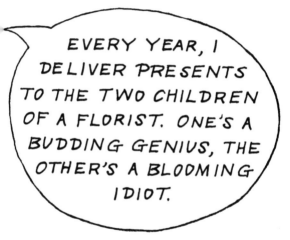

121

Presents Father Christmas can't deliver:

A button for a coat of paint

A saddle for a clothes horse

Sheets for an oyster bed

Music for a
rubber band

False teeth for
a river's mouth

Shoes for a
walking stick

Why does
Father Christmas always
go down chimneys?

**Because it
soots him.**

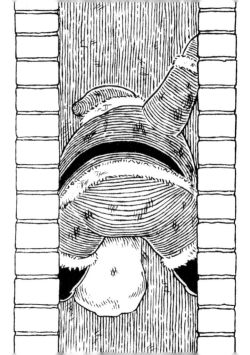